TEENAGE START UP

HOW TO START BUSINESS AS A TEEN

HARSHVARDHAN SINGH

Contents

Foreword

I am delighted to write this foreword, not only because Harshvardhan Singh has been an intern in our company, but also because I deeply believe in his entrepreneurial ability and knowledge. According to the statistics, India is one of the fastest growing economies in the world and it also has a significant youth population. It continues to be a land of opportunities, offering excellent scope for those who want to turn to entrepreneurs.

Entrepreneurship gives young people the ability to work on their skills, interests, and passions. Youth entrepreneurship gains an even bigger significance in the Indian context given its ability to contribute actively to economic development. With an average age of 29 years, India is today among the world's youngest countries. This demographic potential and their inherent entrepreneurial talent translate into an opportunity to address economic and social inequities and thereby drive development and growth.

This book can be a great source of motivation and help for young entrepreneurs who want to start their business at a very early age. Starting a business requires know-how in various fields like finance, legal, technology, marketing and may others. This book is a comprehensive book covering all the essential knowledge to start a business.

Niranjan Hiranandani
Managing Director, Hiranandani Group

Preface

Start Up is a major buzzword now a days and it keeps popping up in the modern education system, whether it is schools, colleges and/ or universities.

Being a business studies student in High school, I also heard this term repeatedly. I have always been enchanted by the workings of different entities and naturally, I wanted to know more about start-ups. I wanted to figure out what could be a start up, how it works, how can one get started. Of course, I went to my elders and people experienced in such matters, but was met with a disheartening "this topic is not for high school students; you are too young for this" statement.

In this era of technology and the internet, it is not difficult to gain knowledge. So, I started my research and collecting as much information as possible and began analysing it for my knowledge. I understood, through my research, that running a business is intriguing, challenging and gruelling.....but it is so satisfying. There are always different aspects to analyse but there is always one common factor at the end of it all – all start-ups need passionate people working behind them to take them to different levels of success.

I applied a lot of the knowledge I had gained towards initiating a small start up of my own and that is how The Economy News was born. It is a news portal that features global happenings related to entrepreneurship, economy, finance, start-ups and more.

As I went through this learning process, I realized that I had collected a significant amount of information and insights that I could share with others who are searching for answers of their own. Basically, I decided to condense my findings into this book!

Start Ups involve gaining knowledge and skill in a variety of different sectors including Laws, Technology, Marketing, Finance and several other. This book is an attempt to collect that knowledge which would be essential for a business or a start up.

The book is designed to get any budding entrepreneur started with the basic information that is needed to begin realizing their dream of building their own start up. The book begins with young entrepreneurs and their journeys. This segment is focussed on highlighting the different ways these young entrepreneurs have solved a problem or realized their passion. Chapter two gives a brief overview of the things and the mindset you would need to get started and build your business. Gain an idea of different possible avenues you can explore for your start up as a young entrepreneur in Chapter three, keeping in mind that there are a lot more ideas to explore.

Chapters four, five and six will take you through the process of market research, business plan and market validation, respectively. Now this process may not be applicable to all start-ups, specially in the beginning phase. However, as an entrepreneur, developing a business plan, doing market research and validation are all important towards the successful development of your business. A significant part of realizing any business is taking ownership and registering it. Chapter seven takes you through an overview of the different entities you may register your business as. Now this process will be different based on your location, so the chapter gives you an overview of the entities in five locations – India, USA, UK, UAE and Singapore. Chapter eight gives insights on ways to develop your team and chapter nine focusses on the development of your product and service.

There are several different emerging technologies that are being talked about globally. Artificial Intelligence (AI) is one that is making a significant impact in almost all sectors and business management. Chapter ten discusses which emerging technologies are significant and how you can explore these areas for your start up. Chapter eleven focusses on the importance of branding, marketing and how you can help your business with the use of different techniques in marketing. Chapter twelve gives you an overview of the energy for your business – funding. This part of the book is solely dedicated to ways of finding the money and raising it.

A lot of it may seem overwhelming at first. It may also feel that you do not need to use all of it. You might not. However, knowledge is power and it is good to have an understanding of the entire process. Remember, Rome was not built in a day. So take your time and explore what you can do as you learn!

I hope this book is beneficial to all future entrepreneurs.

CHAPTER I

Teenage Entrepreneurs

Entrepreneur is term that continues to pop-up everywhere. However, what does it mean to be an entrepreneur? You will find numerous explanations and definitions, especially from other entrepreneurs, simply because their definition will highlight the quality that is most significant in their perception. However, common in those definitions will be the fact that an entrepreneur is a passionate individual who takes things forward (Seems simple enough, right!), working towards realizing an idea they believe in!

Let's expand on this a little more! An entrepreneur is an individual who creates a new business, while taking on the risks and challenges but also enjoying the rewards. The process of setting up a business is known as entrepreneurship. It is usually assumed that an entrepreneur is an innovator, a source of new ideas, goods, services, and business/or procedures. However, it is so much more than the skills and setting up a business....it is also about carrying a mindset which is centred on self-growth, resilience and motivation.

There are several great examples of entrepreneurs in practically every industry, who have done just that. People all over the world have heard about Elon Musk, Bill Gates, J.K. Rowling, Sara Blakely, Jeff Bezos, Mukesh Ambani, Kiran Mazumdar and so many more. They have built their empires on different ideas, such ideas which most people haven't even though of. Really, how many of us have thought of writers as entrepreneurs? However, J.K. Rowling is a world-renowned writer, who has now become a successful producer and director. Few people thought of re-using space rockets, but Elon Musk made it happen. Perhaps, a common factor that is observed in so many of these leaders, is their resilience and passion to continue (in-spite of setbacks) and keep trying again and again and again to realize their vision.

The profile of an entrepreneur is getting redefined – more leadership positions are opening up for people under the age of 30 and even younger, passionate entrepreneurs emerge in the spectrum today. You do NOT have to be of a certain age to get started with your business! Let's meet few Gen-Z entrepreneurs (between ages 10 – 25) that are working on innovative ideas as they establish a name for their business and themselves.

At five years old, Katelynn "Kiki" Hardee found herself struggling to watch people in her school skip their lunch because their parents could not afford to pay for them. So this Vista California native, worked through **Kiki's Kindness Project** by selling cookies and hot cocoa to raise money. Where was this money applied to?

She had found out that the schools in her District had more than USD 600 in school lunch debt. The collected amount was used to pay that. Through her hard work, she has paid off the district's debt her continual efforts for over 2 years has raised more than USD 22000.

Hart Main

Founder of
ManCans

Founder's age
Started at age 13

Scented candles have been a part of gift giving for a long period of time. At age 13, Hart Main came up with the idea to make manly scented candles. Where did this idea come from? It came from sibling fun! Hart Main was teasing his sister for selling "girly" scented candles for one of her school fundraisers. For one of his own passions, when he ended up needing a $1,500 bike, he put that idea to more of a reality.

To start with **ManCans** (clever combination of Man Candles!) , Hart along with his parents, contributed minimal amounts initially. The family worked together as a unit to develop the candles. Currently, ManCans candles are handmade by the Beaver Creek Candle Company in Lisbon, Ohio. The production is run by a developmentally disabled workforce, using soup cans. Primarily focussing on masculine scents like Campfire, Bacon, Sawdust, Fresh Cut Grass, and Grandpa's Pipe, Hart's candles are sold in every state with total revenue bouncing over six figures in USD. Hart believes in overall development of the community and donates a part of EACH sale to different non-profit food serving groups (soup kitchens) in Ohio, Pennsylvania, West Virginia, and Michigan.

Kamaria Warren

Founder of
Brown Girls Stationery

Founder's age
Started at age 7

Let's meet Kamaria Warren. At age seven, Kamaria along with her mother, Shaunice Sasser who specialized in graphic design, went shopping for birthday invitations for her upcoming party. The challenge they encountered was a lack of representation – there were no invitations/products that represented Brown and Black girls. This led to the development of **Brown Girls Stationery.**

It's not just about the stationery. They create party supplies, vegan purses and accessories that feature a fun and uplifting illustration of a Black or Brown Girl. The McDonough, Georgia, native also sells dolls. Although working with people in smaller numbers, the business is growing. Warren sells her products on Shopify, Faire Marketplace, wholesale, and at local events. Each year, on average, Warren ends up selling around 10,000 notebooks, 2,500 notepads, 1,500 backpacks each year. Kamaria finds her motivation through her customers, seeing them be happy wearing her products and feeling represented. Her motto is: Dear Br own girl, you have the ability to change the world.

Ryan Hickman

Founder of
Ryan's Recycling Company

Founder's age
Started at age 7

Ryan Hickman, unhappy with seeing discarded bottles and disposables on the ground, started collecting the recyclables and delivered them to a nearby recycling centre. Getting a return of $5 for each trip, he started collecting the recyclables from his neighbourhood. This expanded to **Ryan's Recycling Company**, which the Orange County, California resident started running by the age of seven.

Hickman has been has been hailed by different news organizations and has appeared on several national TV shows in USA, talking about his mission. Ryan contributes a part of his sales to the rescue organization Pacific Marine Mammal Center. His hard work is paying off, as he has raised more than USD 14,000 and helped recycle 1.5 million cans and bottles. Educating others on the importance of recycling, Hickman has also started a non-profit, **Project 3R.**

Vinusha MK

Founder of
Four Seasons Pastry

Founder's age
Started at age 12

Vinusha MK started **Four Seasons Pastry** in September 2018 after she first tried baking a cake for her mother's birthday. Repeated tries led her to master the skill and love baking. The name of the company denotes seasonal colours and flavours that she focusses on for her cupcakes.

With a vision to teach and impart skills to everyone, Vinusha's vision includes the establishment of an affordable culinary institute in India, allowing easier access for low-income people. She currently sells her unique and delicious treats and a baking kit to help kids bake cakes. Currently selling these treats online, she is also honing in her skills and is an intern under famous chefs in India.

Lily Born

Founder of
**Kangaroo Cup
Imagiroo LLC**

Founder's age
Started at age 8

Eight year old Lily Born invented a three-legged cup which primarily realizes thought that the best way to deal with a spill is to avoid it. The need for the cup arose as she watched her grandfather, a patient of Parkinson's disease frequently spill his beverages, leaving others to clean up the mess. This three legged cup, called the **Kangaroo cup**, does not tip over. Based on this cup, she started her company called **Imagiroo LLC.**

It's not easy to gain a perfect design in the first try, Lily and her dad travelled to China (literally across the world) where they refined the models, found manufacturers and set the production process. Funding is a challenge for any small business and Lily has worked hard to get funding from crowdfunding platforms Kickstarter and Indiegogo. Tens of thousands of Kangaroo cups have been sold worldwide.

***

Michale "Mikey" Wren

Founder of
Mikey's Munchies Vending

Founder's age
Started at age 13

Founder of **Mikey's Munchies Vending**, Michael 'Mikey' Wren always gravitated towards business and finance dealings. In addition to working for his business, at the age of 13, Mikey volunteers his time to teach the more important topics of financial literacy and hosts an annual drive to donate new toys to local kids.

Author of two books, Mikey Learns About Business, which covers writing a business plan, marketing strategies, and networking, and Biz Is a Whiz for children pre-K to 3, Mikey has been sharing his knowledge and skills with everyone.

Moziah Bridges

Founder of
Mo's Bows

Founder's age
Started at age 9

A Memphis, USA native started **Mo's Bows** because at the tender age of nine, he could not find a suitable bowtie. He went through the entire knowledge gaining process by first learning to sew and then by making colourful bowties with leftovers from different sewing projects. Eventually, this expanded to hiring tailors as he managed the creative avenues and the business aspects.

Now over the age of 20, and a Shark Tank participant, Moziah has sold over USD 700,000 in handmade men's ties and accessories. He even had the opportunity to give Barack Obama, former US President, a custom-made tie in "Obama Blue".

Fraser Doherty

Founder of
SuperJam

Founder's age
Started at age 14

Based out of Edinburgh, Scotland, Doherty began making jams from his grandmother's recipes at the age of 14. Deciding to sell his jams at the local farmers market opened up orders for him, which he delivered using his bike. The quality of the product was great and resulted in him receiving greater number of orders....more than he had time to fulfil. It was at this point where he decided to drop out of school and rent a factory to meet that demand. His business continues to grow as the jams were picked up by supermarket Waitrose in 2007. These products are now also available in Korea and Japan. Queen Elizabeth II awarded Fraser an MBE medal which is for his services to business in the UK. In 2019, Fraser sold his 5 millionth jar of jam! He continually runs community projects for the elderly as well as beekeeping projects.

Divya Gandotra Tandon

Founder of
TheScoopBeats

Founder's age
Started at age 18

The 18 year old YouTuber Divya entered the business world. Wanting to share all that she was learning about the most up-to-date and popular technology in the market, Divya started uploading videos on her YouTube account to help people understand what they are purchasing. Through this, she founded **TheScoopBeats** which is a news and media organisation.

Having gained popularity on different social media platforms, more than 90,000 individuals of all ages follow TheScoopBeats. Moreover, she is an influencer on Instagram and is working hard to change the lives of other as well. A multi talented young entrepreneur, she is has experience in domains such as celebrity management, social media management, and online influence.

***

Mia Monzidelis

Founder of
Power Pony

Founder's age
Started at age 5

Tackling the desire of little kids to want ponies, specially while living in a big city, Mia came up with the idea of **Power Pony**. Primarily started because she herself was denied to own a pony at age 5 (it would be extremely challenging to have a pony at their house in Bellmore, Long Island, New York), Mia came up with the idea of a mechanical pony or unicorn that was made with a furry surface. The entire operation of the pony is interactive and has an iOS app.

The four-legged toys can travel around the room with a child riding in the saddle. The dimension of the toy are quite manageable - 20 inches from the ground to the saddle and 16 inches from the footpads to the saddle. It is 24 inches long from the handle to the tail. Encouraged by her parents but more so by her dad, Monzidelis said they sampled many pony toys before they struck on the right one. She says it was a frustrating process to have to keep looking for what they needed, but definitely rewarding once they achieved it. Power Pony is continually growing with 15 employees and 12 volunteers. The sales are up with notable numbers in the 2021 holiday season. "I have always helped kids and families that are in need in whatever way I could, and now with Power Pony, I can help so many kids that are sick or need help," she says. Mia donates a significant amount to charities and those in need.

Tilak Mehta

Founder of
Paper and Parcels

Founder's age
Started at age 13

Tilak Mehta is one of the **young entrepreneurs in India** who believes in the spirit of curiosity to try something different to build something extraordinary from the ordinary. Mehta is the founder of an app-based courier service in Mumbai, called **Paper and Parcels**. A digital courier company which provides one-day parcel services.

The unique part is that it collaborates with Mumbai Dabbawalas (Tiffin/lunch box transporters delivering food from homes to offices/ different locations). His company ensures same day delivery within Mumbai and offers a different earning option to the Dabbawalas. The company offers door-to-door pickup and delivery services for everything from a pen to paperwork, and lunch. On a daily basis, it delivers roughly 1200 parcels to their destinations on the same day.

You can find out more about these entrepreneurs (and others) from easy web searches (that is how this information was collected!). In the process of learning about these young entrepreneurs, there are a few impactful revelations. What are the important (almost common to all) points are here?

- Ideas can come from anywhere – can be simple enough
- Realization of ideas requires passion and dedication
- Skills needed to start and run a business can be developed by anyone
- Things may not work the first time around.....but failure (and the fear of it), should not be the end of your passion!
- Work the problem – the first solution may not be the best one. Continue to evaluate and explore possibilities of improvement.

All of these individuals have continually worked passionately towards their ideas, in-spite of setbacks and failures. It is okay to be afraid of failing at your idea but that in no way should mean that you give up on your goal to become an entrepreneur. After all,

"Courage is not the absence of fear, but is doing something in-spite of it. "

It is very important to always remember that no entrepreneur is born with all the needed skills. Few skills may already inherently be present in a person but they can also be developed. A resourceful entrepreneur

- Can honestly understand and accept their existing skillset.
- Does not hesitate in developing new skills as needed.
- Works dedicatedly towards their idea and what they believe in.
- Is not discouraged by challenges and failures, but learns from them and tries again.

Entrepreneurship doesn't always mean that you HAVE TO be the most knowledgeable person in that industry. You can see from all the entrepreneurs listed here, that it's more about inspiration, and ideation which leads to realization of a business!

How can one get started towards their entrepreneurship journey?

It requires being mindful of few essential aspects to get ready to jump into becoming a businessperson – everything ranging from idea building, team management, finances to market research, product development and more.

This book will talk about all aspects as it goes further on. Remember, it is a continuous learning process.

Let's get started!

CHAPTER II

Getting Started for the Start Up

Let's talk about the essentials. As one looks to get started with building their own venture, let's talk about the key things that are needed to begin this journey.

First things first, find an idea based on which the start up will be developed! As discussed, no one has all the necessary skills from the get go. However, it is important to know the skills that you need and the roadmap to develop them. Keep in mind, that your work and your skill development may happen in parallel, meaning you learn as you are working towards building your start up.

Other essentials that entrepreneurs need more than others maybe are motivation, passion and commitment.

Finding your Start Up idea!

Every entrepreneurial journey is different. For some, the idea that they want to work on is obvious and easy to find. For others, it takes time to evaluate what/which area they want to work in. You know what? Both of these paths are correct!

There are several examples of how a simple idea can grow into a start up, it's a matter of finding that idea and then working on it. There are different ways to come up with this idea. However, broadly classifying, let's talk about two such ideas.

Observe and identify

In our everyday lives, you encounter several events and situations that can raise certain issues/ flags in your minds. Observe what is happening around you and make note of situations and circumstances or tasks that may benefit from an upgradation. There is an organized way of doing this. Simply create a list of things that you feel may be improved or require a modification. In this list, also include possible solutions. See if an interesting possibility exists in those solutions and look in on that idea to see if you can develop it further.

" "Need is the mother of all invention" "

You may be the next inventor that is able to solve a challenging problem that a lot of people are dealing with.

Follow your area of interests

Another way to search for an idea for your venture is to explore your own hobbies and interests. It is often said that if your profession is in an area that is from your hobbies, then you are bound to achieve a greater level of satisfaction from it. Automatically, the efficiency goes to its highest possible level. So, what is it that you enjoy doing? Playing video games, participating in sports activities, creating products through creative processes like arts and crafts.... or something else entirely.

Keep in mind that this is just the idea development part. Once the idea is there, the next step is to work on developing processes and ways to bring that idea into reality, which is one of the greatest parts about this progression.

Exploring skills – what we have and what we need to develop!

As you start your venture, there are different types of skills that one needs. These include the skills which may be related to the product or service that you plan to provide. However, there are a few skills that all entrepreneurs should at least be comfortably knowledgeable in.

For any venture, both **leadership and managerial roles** are significantly important. What's the difference in the two? While both roles involve supervisory tasks, leadership is a blend of skills that allow one to motivate, console, encourage, and most importantly, inspire a group of people to carry out certain tasks towards a common goal.

Managerial roles are what keep the company moving. It involves creating and streamlining processes, create the rules and regulations that would be needed and to work towards achieving the aims/goals of the company.

Now entrepreneurship is a healthy blend of both – leadership skills and managerial/management skills. Leadership to provide direction and management to provide set systems that allow the venture to keep growing.

The role and skills of an entrepreneur are not set in stone.

The most common underlying feature, however, remains the passion that the entrepreneur has for their venture and people.

Getting started with one's own business involves understanding as well as dealing with different issues such as finance, problem solving, sales, marketing, human resources and much more. So, if this list is quantified, then it may be categorized into the following key segments about which a young entrepreneur should know.

1. **<u>Creative thinking</u>**

   This is all about thinking outside the box. This becomes helpful in developing new tasks, strategies, solving problems and challenges. It may include analytical, open-minded, and problem-solving skills along with organization and communication skills.

2. **<u>Effective Communication</u>**

   Communication that involves exchanging ideas, opinions, sharing knowledge, discussing/solving conflict – all done with a purpose and clarity. Now this communication may be verbal and/or written, in person or online/telephonically.

3. **<u>Financial Knowledge</u>**

   Finances are the backbone of any venture. Strong financial knowledge helps with making informed choices in terms of when to spend/purchase and invest.

4. **<u>Time Management</u>**

This is an important skill. Entrepreneurs need to appreciate the significance of time and its management. The skill is all about organizing and planning on how to divide your time for different activities. Now let's scale that up for our venture. Time management here talks about the organizing and planning for carrying out different tasks that result in efficient working environments.

5. **<u>Flexibility</u>**

Flexibility in an entrepreneur is a key skill. As mentioned earlier in this book, an entrepreneur ends up taking care of multiple things. So flexibility and openness to take care of different tasks (even in areas that one may not be too fond of) is important.

Flexibility, to some extent, also requires knowledge or access to knowledgeable people that may help with the process of achieving a task.

6. **<u>Technical Skills</u>**

These are more custom skills that are related specifically to the venture. For example, someone who is planning to open a venture related to e-commerce or physical exercise, will need to know respective relevant technical information.

Research, Sales and Marketing are all important skills to evaluate here.

7. **<u>Multi-Tasking</u>**

Relating back to flexibility, the ability to do more than one task, and then to be able to do several significant tasks at the same time, are important skills.

Now, it may seem a bit overwhelming to go through these skills. If you created a checklist in your brain to see which skills you possess, that's good. Now think of how you can develop the skills where you feel you are lagging (or find people who can help).

The motivation and commitment needed.

On a little bit of a serious note, it is important for budding entrepreneurs (actually all entrepreneurs) to realize that starting a venture is a long-term commitment. It requires consistency, resilience, motivation and long hours dedicated towards achieving goals.

Several challenges pop up for every passionate entrepreneur that is venturing into starting something innovative of their own.

Do you need to know what these challenges are?
ABSOLUTELY!

Do you need to back down because of them?
ABSOLUTELY NOT!

Once you are aware of what the challenges may be, you will be better prepared to deal with them and in most cases, be able to anticipate them! The appropriate proverb here is **"knowing is half the battle"**. Once you know of the challenges, you are able to make informed decisions and develop solutions.

Here they are – the more common challenges that all entrepreneurs have faced in one way or another:

- Developing and ideating a unique product or service – This is definitely the most common and the biggest challenge! But, it is also the most fun one to tackle. It takes you towards exploring new things, applying creative solutions and discovering new things about yourself!
- Clear vision of what you want your start-up/ product to be
- Developing a strong business plan
- Figuring out how to get sufficient flow of money (sufficient capital and cash flow)
- Finding a great team. Building a great team and keeping them is one of the biggest challenges that you face as the venture's leader. It is worth it though. The right team can propel your venture in high speed towards achieving targets and foals.

- You know what's a bigger challenge? Letting people go (firing them) to increase efficiency and productivity but doing it in such a way that does not result in any legal backlash
- Admitting there is a need to modify the current strategy and to pivot from it based on supporting information.
- Putting in more and more work than you expected (this is a tricky one!).
- Applying time management skills. As leaders, it is easier to preach but challenging to follow time management advice. However, that is just it. You lead by first doing it yourself.
- At the same time, it is important to maintain a work/life balance (yes it exists – good time management will lead you to it)
- The biggest challenge of all time? – To keep going in spite of customer rejections, conflicts and one or more of the previous challenges. Keeping your own motivation and drive high is a big challenge.

Motivation to continue is key. As the leader, you have the amazing responsibility to ensure your team has the motivation to continue. So, find your motivators – family, friends, loved ones OR just sheer passion for what you do and believe in. Know that everyone faces failure and challenges but also know that there are options to recover from it.

Remember, generating an idea is the first step, a more significant one is to actually move forward with it and start working towards making it a reality. Your skill set and process do not need to be perfect before you begin your entrepreneurial journey. Just make the move to get started!

The right passion and drive will carry you through the biggest of challenges. Just take the next step and jump into it!

DON'T DELAY IT....JUST DO IT!

CHAPTER III

Think a Business Idea

Starting your entrepreneurial journey as a teen can be a very rewarding and worthwhile experience. It is a great process to develop leadership and management skills as you step closer to the adult world. With the different tasks that you end up managing (school, hobbies, social life), along side your own venture, you end up developing multi-tasking and time management skills that are crucial for life.

As one is starting out in entrepreneurship it may be more manageable to choose a start up idea that offers more options for a flexible schedule and requires minimal experience, specially considering the existing time commitments.

There are several areas where teens can explore different ideas for start-ups. Few are suggested here that are quite prominent and are easier to set up and manage.

1. Blogger/ Opinion/ News Blog

Begin with a blogging start up as you share your interests, thoughts and ideas with others. This type of a start up requires basic writing skills. Now you can carry this out in different ways. A blogging start up may be a website that is dedicated primarily to your writings, or it can be a collaborative venture, that allows other budding and freelance writers to contribute and reduces your challenges (a little bit). You just have to make sure the collaboration stays on theme of your blog.

2. Ecommerce

Most people have heard the term E-Commerce and it refers to selling of different goods.....basically an online store. As you think about setting up your E-Commerce start up, keep in mind the type of store you would like it to be. Honestly, it can be anything for which there is a demand.

It is a rewarding business that gives you the opportunity to connect consumers and sellers.

3. Freelance Content Writing/ Designing

Thinking of putting your existing skills as freelance writer to good use? Then you can become a freelance content writer and offer services to businesses, publications and direct to clients for creating customized content for their products (product descriptions), website content, press release articles, news articles, blog posts and so much more.

As a freelance writer, you would have options to connect with as many and few potential clients and maintain flexibility in your work. There are a number of online platforms that offer connection options for freelancers.

4. Online/ Offline Tutoring

Everyone is looking for people to help with their learning processes. Use what skills and knowledge you have gained through your schooling and help others through tutoring business. Offering these services online, gives an opportunity to reach a bigger customer base.

Of course, to keep it manageable with your existing schedule, it may be best to start offline. This business allows you to charge by the hour or by subject, or both!

5. Become a Social Media Influencer

Now here is a term which is very popular and in high demand. Becoming a social media influencer primarily requires you to understand how to effectively create and market a brand. The source of revenue for social media influencers is brand deals or sponsorships collaborations with different brands.

More and more social media platforms are encouraging influencer visibility. If you can generate a large following/ viewership in a specific sector/industry, specially if you have a passion for it, then SMI is a great start up idea for you.

6. Food Truck

A food truck gives a creative avenue to express your food creativity with basic cooking skills and lets you travel to different locations – schools, parties, community events and get togethers. You have the option to start out small – food cart or stand at local events and go from there!

You would have the freedom to partner up with an expert in the genre of food or get a team of peers together.

7. Podcasting

What is Podcasting? A podcast is an audio program that is available for download. The popularity of podcasts on variety of topics is increasing every day. The most successful podcasts include latest topics along with enthusiastic/ engaging hosts.

If you are comfortable with holding discussions, interviewing people and public speaking, then podcasting may be a great option for you. Podcasting is a direct start up that allows you to bring the issues that matter to you most, to the forefront. For example, you want to talk about global warming, your podcast can do features with environmentalists, sustainability experts and so much more.

8. Start Up on Etsy

If you are a creator of customized handicrafts, unique goods, selling them on Etsy is a way to reach a large customer base. Setting up on Etsy is easy and it automatically takes care of setting up your payment options and catalogues of your beautiful creations.

9. Babysitting/ Housesitting/ Pet sitting Business

A classic business idea in some countries. Depending on which country you are in, you may have to check up on rules and regulations to carry this business out. Mostly, this business is dependent on you trustworthiness and experience with children and pets. What do I mean by that? The owners/parents must trust you and be comfortable enough to allow you to take responsibility of the important ones in their lives.

This start up again may be charged by the hour, and the number of entities you are taking care of.

10. Showcase your Photography

Passion in photography can lead to a profitable start up idea. Not only does it let you showcase your creativity through photography, you can either directly sell prints of your photos or become a photographer for hire. Both options give you an opportunity to hone in your skills.

Also, you can earn from selling your photos as stock images on websites like Pexels, iStock etc...

11. Graphic Design

Graphic Designers find their business through creating visual branding that may be used on products and/or marketing materials. May require skill development in the latest techniques and styles. However, the skills are applicable to different sectors of industry. Think in terms of things like logo design, web design, book cover layout etc... Graphic designers are needed by businesses in all industries.

12. Game Creation

Okay now this one here is extra interesting. You can look at game creation – online or offline (board games). Are you Tech – Savvy, then online game creation may be your area in which you can begin work. Apply your creativity and skills to create online games that may be utilized on different devices. Of course, for aspects requiring engineering or computer science backgrounds, you may collaborate with others.

13. App Development

Similar to Game Creation, App Development requires a little bit of tech-savviness. New apps keep popping up every day. You may think "There's an App for that", but in actuality its more "There's an App for that.... but it could be better". Always room to add more features and improve performance. This means there is always scope in App Development.

You can work on either developing your own app or offer consultancy services to others that may want a customized App development. Keep in mind, this is only about Mobile Apps right now but there are also Web Apps (like Webex etc...) to develop.

14. Tech Support

Establish yourself as the tech guru. A Tech Support business, like many on this list, can be started from your home. The marketing for the same can be done through flyers, other local business (also a great customer base). The business may be run from any location of convenience and again you have the option to charge by the hour or specifically by the job.

Get/ Stay connected with your potential client base digitally through e-mail or social media platforms.

15. YouTube Channel

Getting your YouTube channel set up is easy! All you need is an active email account. The platform offers exclusive tools and video content creation options. There are different types of videos that you can share and increase your followers. The content can be education based, training on skills like painting, crafts, mathematics, or it can also be video blogging (vlogging).

There are a number of ways you can work on YouTube. With its new feature of Shorts, you don't have to limit yourself towards only creating longer videos. Talk directly to the people, teach them something, or share your work/travel experience through your YouTube channel.

Now, there are ideas that may be added to this list because the list is endless. There are a lot of ways to get started with your business idea. Remember, you can mainly focus on utilizing the skills you have or channelize your energy to developing an idea in areas where you are passionate.

CHAPTER IV

Do Market Research

You have figured out what you want to do and how you want to do it (mostly) – Congratulations! You are on your way to getting started with your own start up.

The next steps focus on figuring out whether people will want to buy what you are selling. This may be reasoned through **Market Research**!

Let's understand what Market Research is.

Formally, market research is the process which results in collecting information about your start up's practicality and sustainability in the market along with a better understanding of your potential customers. Market research allows for the following:

- Understand how the product or service solves a problem for the customers.
- Explore how many people currently face a similar challenge – they are the potential client base, i.e., the people you would be directly offering the service to. They form the potential **market size**.
- Evaluate other companies that are offering solutions to the same problems. This is **identification and analysis** of your competitors.
- Develop and evaluate a **stepwise methodology** on how you can **reach your potential customer** and sell your product/service – directly or through marketing channels like a website or social media or word of mouth.

Simply put, market research allows you to understand the potential customer, the fit of the product, service to the demands of the customer and how the competitor's products or services measure up to what you have to offer.

How do I get market research information for my business?

Before gaining access to the information, first understand what different features and information is needed. Generally, the first step is to form predictions that would be important, called as **hypotheses** – they formulate the key questions. Once you have your hypotheses (basically, the questions you want answered), the next step is to approach different avenues to obtain answers to these questions.

Okay, next step. Let's talk about the type of information that you may use to conduct the research. This information is collected from different sources. Mainly, these are segmented into 2: Primary and Secondary.

If you gain this information directly by interacting with potential customers (target market), this is called **Primary Research**. It helps in market segmentation as well as product enhancement. It may be carried out through: Surveys, Questionnaires, Focus groups, in-depth interviews, social media polls.

Some people may not want to share personal information and may be more comfortable giving responses anonymously.

Be aware though: The greater is the number of anonymous responses, more challenging it will be to **trust** the validity of the data. That is something to be careful about when collecting blind data (where you cannot directly interact with the person).

You're probably thinking that collecting all this data first-hand is going to be time consuming, and right you are!

This is where **Secondary Research** becomes useful. You can use pre-collected data like industry reports, public database and publicly shared survey/questionnaire results to get information on the questions you need answered.

So which type of data is better for which kind of research?

If you are looking at **broader analysis** – meaning you are trying to gain an overview of the market trends and gain a general outlook, then you can begin the analysis with secondary research, i.e. the data which already exists.

However, for a more **detailed and targeted approach**, you may need primary research as well. This will require identification of people that you would like to get information from and devising methods that will allow to connect with them and gain the information.

Once you have the data, now what? **Organize and analyse** this data to gain insights that will allow you to answer the questions in your hypotheses! Analysis of the data may require skills that you need to brush up on. Of course, you can talk to people who may be knowledgeable and would be able to help with the analysis.

What should I be looking at while I conduct market research?

Start Simple! Figure out the following:

1. Is there a demand for your product/ service? If so, how big is that demand? Has it grown in the past few months? What is your customer's pain point (aka what do they need)?
2. What is the size of the target market, i.e., how many people are interested in buying your product/service?
3. Competition and Saturation – How many similar options are available? How are they different from your solution? Understanding competition and saturation help you to evaluate your potential market share (percentage of sales made by a business in a specific industry/sector). The number of competitors and similar products or services are sometimes called as players in the market.
4. Once you have figured out the market share and the remainder of the competitive landscape, evaluate in terms of:

   a. Their strengths and weaknesses.
   b. Where does your window of opportunity to jump-in lies.

c. What may stop you? What barriers would you have to find solutions to?

d. Competitors who may directly/indirectly impact your product/service

This seems too much – Do I have to do this much Market Research to get started with something of my own?

Simply put, no you don't. You can take that first step to get started right now.

However, continual Market Research is important for any and every business, not just start ups. A properly conducted market research allows you to understand and reduce the risks involved, even at the beginning stages.

There will rarely be a "0 risk" situation or business.... That is correct.

With Market Analysis though, you have the option to identify challenging areas, either in your target market or production, and devise solutions on how to resolve or minimize those risks.

Not to mention though, Market Research also helps you identify the existing customer base and a competitor's analysis gives you an insight on the directions you can take to improve your product/ service. Another outcome of carrying out market research is that it gives insights into possible pricing strategies. **Target market's demand/ feedback and competitor trends** are directive indicators towards service modification. The steps may seem tedious, but really, once you begin, the market research process is invigorating, challenging and a learning experience.

CHAPTER V

Write a Business Plan

Business Plan is an important document to have ready for your company as it details different aspects about the products, services the goals, and the steps. Basically, it is a guide that explains what 52 goal is, what you want to do to achieve that goal, and how you want to do it, i.e. it details

i. Goals
ii. Tasks to achieve the goal
iii. Roadmap to finish tasks

All companies, whether start up or established businesses, use business plans. This document not only contains the goals and the process plans, but also the roadmap for financial, marketing and operational processes.

It is important for few key reasons:

- A business plan keeps the team in a company on the same page regarding short-term and long-term objectives
- It is a handy tool that helps in acquiring funding – whether that is through external investors or through credit lines and bank loans (Don't worry...the book will touch up on these terms in later sections!)

A good business plan may be lengthy or short. However, it should be clear and precise on the key points that need to be conveyed. In general, a business plan includes the following:

- An executive summary
- Details of the Products/ Services
- Market research and analysis

- Marketing/Branding Strategies
- Financial Plans
- Budgeting (what to do with the money)

So, what are the steps to getting your business plan ready? Let's go through it:

1. **Write your executive summary!**
   Although it is given here as the first step, it is usually easier to write it last! It is a summary of the major aspects of your company. This includes the mission, the goals, products and services, your financial growth plans and marketing techniques. Of course, all of this is described in brief in the executive summary.

2. **About the Company**
   Literally, this is talking about your company! Share details on the registered name, its location (address) and the names of the key people in the business, while highlighting their unique skills and experiences. Now you may not have all these aspects defined and clarified in your mind – that is absolutely alright. The goals of developing the business plan is to get you thinking and to get organized for your business.

   As a new business, you may not have figured out all of the roles and positions in the business. However, the main roles that are defined for any start up as it grows, are C-level which includes Chief Executive Officer (CEO), Chief Technology Officer (CFO), Chief Operations Officer (COO), Chief Technology Officer (CTO), Chief Marketing Officer (CMO), Chief Human Resources Officer (CHRO). Again, you do NOT have to start out with all of these positions filled.

3. **Business Mission and Goals**
   Define your objective! Explain the short-term and long-term goals for the start up. When applying for financial assistance, this segment is where you can share how funds will be utilized

to achieve the goals and meet targets.

4. **Services and products of your start up**
   Now this section is dedicated entirely to the core of your work –
   your service or product. In an organized way, share the details.
   It may include (but is not limited to):

   - What the products or services are.
   - How they work and their uniqueness
   - The client base – the type of customer you serve
   - Sales and distribution strategies
   - The production and supply chain process
   - Any intellectual property (IP) associated with the business (the
     book will talk about IP soon as well!)

5. **Showcase primary points of your market research**
   You have already done market research to check product
   viability. Now think about how you would want to showcase
   it so that investors and lenders are convinced about how your
   product sets you apart from the competition. This section may
   also detail the competitors and explain why your services/
   products are better.

6. **Detail out your marketing and sales plans**
   Marketing and sales are focused on convincing people to avail
   your products, services. Layout who your target customer is and
   how you plan to reach them through different traditional and/or
   digital marketing and sales avenues.

7. **Perform financial analysis and projections**
   As a start up, one may feel that they don't need to maintain
   business financials, but it is important to start this habit as soon
   as you finalize the decision of starting your start up. Now you
   may not be able to include it in the business plan, but a balance
   sheet and a list of assets and debts will be key inputs here.

Projections are based on existing records and data for sales, profits and losses. Now as you start out, these will not be available However, this section will keep a record of the expenses/revenues (no matter how big or small) which will give the opportunity to analyse and make projections for the future.

Terms like **Net profit margin** (the percentage of revenue that one can keep their income), **current ratio** (the ability to pay off debts), **accounts receivable turnover ratio** (frequency of collecting income from receivables per year) are all important to perform financial analysis and detail projections.

8. **Supporting material**
   This is the appendix and basically includes and supporting information, references or data that may help a third person gain insights into your business.

Is it not easier to see why the executive summary is written last? Since it is a summary of all the different aspects of the company, it is far easier to write out everything else first and then summarize the key points into the Executive Summary.

Now if writing the business plan seems to be a daunting task, then you can always take help. However, even though there are services and templates available online that can ease this task, it is highly recommended that you go through this process on your own for few key reasons:

- **Clarity** - since it is your start up and idea, you tend to know everything about it. When you write out the different aspects of a business plan, you will go into minute details that bring about clarity for the reader and the team.
- **Unique Vision** – Your idea and the way you want to carry it out, is a creative process. When you are building on unique ideas and processes, detailing them out yourself is a good way to check the feasibility of the plans.

Summarizing, the existing templates are a good source of references and ideas on how to write the business plan, but you do not need to follow them strictly. Do not confine yourself to the generic but showcase the start up's one-of-kind plan.

CHAPTER VI

Market Validation

Now this seems to be a pretty daunting term, but it is not! Market validation is simply a process that allows to figure out if there is a need for the product/service in the market, i.e. whether the customers will buy it or not. This consequently answers the question of whether the business would be profitable.

This is an important step to take initially simply to ensure that

- You and your team do not misallocate time and resources on a product that may not be a good fit.
- The market validation is a great motivator for investors and lenders to trust the continuity of your product and to invest in it.
- As the owner, you gain a more in-depth understanding of who your target customers are, how you can engage with them and address their needs.

Through validation, you end up asking the following key questions:

- What value do I offer through my product/service?
- Who is my target customer? What do I know about them?
- What separates the product/service from similar ones that are already in the market?
- What are the assumptions and predictions related to the product, pricing and business models?

Generally, you can follow few steps to obtain market validation on a service or a product. Now the steps (and sub-steps) may be different according to the start up industry and the product that you want to validate but here is more of a general idea of the steps that may be followed. The primary goal is to understand how well the products or services will be received by the customer base.

1. **Create a simple explanation of your product and service idea/ concept**
   Develop an explanation that is easy to understand for majority of the people and not just those who are directly linked to the design and development of the service/ product. Remember, your customer may not understand extremely technical terms and would need simpler explanations.

   For example, if your product is a new phone attachment that helps you take astronomical photos, then you have to describe this product such that non-astronomy lovers would still understand its utility.

   Include details on the problems that are being faced and how your product would solve it.

2. **Identify your target customer base**
   On occasion, there is a vague idea of who is likely to buy the products/ services. In this case, start with a quick understanding of how they respond.

   However, sometimes it is important explore more areas and explore in detail who the target base is.

3. **Narrow down the questions you want to ask your target clients**
   The way you ask a question, makes all the difference. Keep your questions to your clients clear and direct. Since the goal of the market validation is to understand if the product/service tackles a need/problem in the market, it may help to frame your questions that **highlight the problem** rather than those focussing on your product.

4. **Ask all the questions!**
   Now you can conduct in-depth interviews with your target

population and give them time to really answer the questions. The more they have the freedom to analyse the question, greater are the chances that a more accurate description of their problem will come up.

5. **Evaluate all the answers (Deal with the Data!)**

So, what exactly do you look for in the hopefully sufficient amount of data that you have collected? Patterns that may highlight one or more of the following:

- Your service/product tackles an area or provides such a solution that the market would pay to resolve.
- The target client base is yet to discover another solution to this problem (best case scenario) or that the target client base is not entirely satisfied with the existing solutions (more likely).
- The primary industries that deal with the problems are actually willing to spend some money to address the problem.

6. **Present the data**

After evaluating the data and drawing your conclusions, present them in a clear, concise, and easy to understand format. Design it according to the people who will read it.

Do you feel that Market Validation is not immediately a need for your business? You know, you may be correct. Market validation seems to be a viable need for start ups that are selling a physical product, whether online or offline. However, if you are doing a service based start up, do you still need validation?

So, the overall answer is yes, you do need market validation. However, your way of obtaining that market validation may be different. Take any food delivery service as an example. It is providing a service that addresses a need for the customers (a large client base). Without a need for people wanting their food to be delivered in an easy manner, these services would not be profitable.

What about something like babysitting/house sitting/ pet sitting? So think about how you would gain validation here. Since these services are more locally centred, your client base is your neighbourhood. Based on the people who live there, you would be able to figure out if a particular service is needed. When you are scaling your business up to address a larger area, then your market validation would need to be modified so that you can answer questions of financial nature.

It is to note that, the general validation process gives an idea of what may be done to obtain the answer to the question of "Whether my product/service is needed?" but the process of carrying out the research varies. Just as the definition of entrepreneurs is evolving, so is this process of market validation. Evaluate how your start up idea would need to be validated in today's market!

CHAPTER VII

Register Your Business

So far, the book has discussed different aspects that are needed in terms of planning and getting started. At this point, the business plan is developed, market research is done and there is an overall understanding of how the product is expected to perform with the target client base. Launching the business and getting it registered are processes that are a requirement for an authorized launch of the start up.

This launch is to increase the visibility of your business. Now this is carried out in two ways: 1) Legal Entity Registration and consequent legal matters 2) Online visibility through business domain registration.

Before you begin with the registration processes, you need a name for the start up! Generally, business website domains match with the name of the actual start up/company EXACTLY. This is easy to remember and usually also allows the visitors to remember what the company does.

Finding a name for your company

A very important task as it ultimately is the way people will recognize your product and your start up. Can the name be anything? Yes. However, it will represent you and your company for a significant amount of time so don't rush into the process. There are a few things to keep in consideration as you search for your start up's name.

1. 3S's – Short, Simple, easy to Spell
In general, consumers are more likely to remember a shorter name,

that is easier to spell in comparison to a big one. Think of major companies like Apple, Nike, Amazon and others. Their names are simple, short, and easy to remember. Of course, the name you choose does not need to be as short as these examples. However, an average of about 15 characters is an appropriate length.

2. Domain availability

A domain name is the address of the website of the start up. The most popular extension (suffix) for websites is *.com*. There are other options available like .io, .news, .net, .org. However, if your company's name is *MyStartUp*, then people are more likely to automatically go to *MyStartUp.com* than any other extension. Therefore, if you can find a name that does not already have a website associated with it in *.com* extension, then it will be better overall. You can check the availability of the name on any domain service company like *GoDaddy.com or Name.com.*

3. Social Media Handles

This book talks about the importance of social media in one of the later sections in the book. In short, the availability of social media handles that match your company name will be a help in marketing and branding of the company. You can easily search for the name on Instagram, Facebook, LinkedIn, Pinterest and see if pages exist with the same name.

4. Legal Registration and Trademark availability

In order to legally register your company, the name that you have chosen must be unique, i.e. no other company should be registered with the same name.

With all this said, do remember that these are general guidelines more than anything else. You do not have to spend excessive amounts of time to finalize the name. Name your start up what you think is the best one for it! It is your company after all.

Register Your Business Domain

Let's quickly go over how you can register your domain name and what it really is. The global list of domain names is maintained by a non-profit called **Internet Corporation for Assigned Named and Numbers (ICANN)**. Now, the ICANN allows other companies to act as Domain Registrars to sell and manage domain names. To register your domain, you may go through any of the many options on domain providers. However, the most common ones are GoDaddy, Bluehost, Name.com, Domain.com. Once the domain is registered, no other entity (private, public, individual, or company) would be able to register the same name as their domain.

The steps to get your domain name are easy to follow:

1. Choose your domain name registrar
2. Select and finalize the name that you want to register with
3. Check whether the domain name is available.
4. Decide on the duration of the registration and a budget for it.
5. Purchase the domain name through your chosen domain name registrar
6. Add protection for your domain to maintain privacy.
7. Make the payment!

Few things to note:

- If the domain name is already registered, then you may purchase it from the current owner if they are open to selling it. However, this can be more expensive than the amount you may have allotted for domain purchasing.
- Also, this may consume more time as it requires going through the owner's domain registrar.
- In this case, it may be easier to consider a different domain name or a different extension (suffix).

- This is a recurring charge. The domain will be registered for you/your company for the duration that you registered and paid for. This service is to be renewed, once the selected duration (point 4 above) is over. You can set it up for autorenewal.

It is to note, that you can register your domain for free on different services like Wix, Weebly, Wordpress, Bluehost, GoDaddy, Freenom and others. This also takes care of the hosting services. However, the resulting domain may also include the name of the service provider.

For example, if you opt for the free domain service through Wix and you want the domain to be *mystartup.com*, then it would actually register as: *mystartup.wixsite.com* . Similarly, on Wordpress this would be, *mystartup.wordpress.com.*

If you need a basic website that is temporary, then the free service is a great option. However, the paid domain names bring about a level of professionalism and transparency to the start up. Moreover, the domain will promote brand development and growth.

Why do you need to do legal registration?

The first thought is usually to continue with the start up idea in its simplest form. It is more convenient and has less obligations that have to be fulfilled. However, registering yourself as a legal entity allows you to build trust.

As a start up begins, it generally approaches within its first contacts – family, friends, friends of friends and so on. There is an inherent trust that follows to your customer. Now, as your start up continues to grow, you will want to increase its reach beyond the initial circle. A registered entity offers that trust building in this case. Similar function would be carried out by your website. Both registrations increase your visibility and build trust through transparency.

Legal Entity Registration

Now the focus is on the different legal entities you can register your start up as and how to finish that process. The legal registration requirements may be different based on the country where you are starting and planning to register your business. The overall steps are similar and that is what the focus will be on.

Alright, let's first understand what a legal entity is. Basically, any person (individual) or group of people, or an organization that has been formed and has legal rights as well as obligations, is called as a legal entity. Among other things, the obligations are directly related to agreements, contracts, payments and penalties. A legal entity is formed based on the regulations of the governing body of the country.

In addition to learning about the different legal entities, one should also understand a few terms. First such term is **Shares**. Phrases of "shares being sold" etc on the stock exchange are fairly commonly heard. Basically, for any company, the shares represent ownership in that company. As and when any individual buys shares of a company, they become one of its owners. The shareholders are the ones that run the company. Another term commonly used is **stakeholders** which represents a person with a concern towards the performance of the organization.

Yet another important term is **equity**, which is basically the value that is returned to the company's shareholders, if the assets of the company were liquidated and any/all debts were paid off in entirety. In other words, it represents their stake or ownership in the company, as identified on the balance sheet. It is calculated as total assets minus the total liabilities.

There can be different types of legal entities that may be formed for your start up. Each country across the globe has different but similar classifications and names. The best way to go about identifying which entity you want to register for is to understand the how large-scale or small-scale you want to aim for. Here is a brief overview of the entities you can register yourself as, in different countries.

<u>India</u>

According to India's Company Law, start ups/ businesses may register as the following legal entities.

- **Private Limited Company (Pvt. Ltd.)**
  Ownership is private and may be formed with a minimum of two (2) members, called as Directors. Maximum number may vary based on location. The losses/profits/debts are to be managed based on the agreements formed between the primary members or the board of directors. This type of company may NOT make or accept deposits from the public. The shares of a private company are not freely transferable.
- **Public Limited Company**
  The securities of a public company may be traded on a stock market and the shares are freely transferable. Since the company is in a public domain, there are more rules and regulations that have to be followed by the owners. Minimum number of people required is generally 7 (may vary based on location).
- **Sole Proprietorship**
  Simplest form under which an individual may operate. Now the proprietorship itself is not a legal entity, but the person who has started the business becomes personally responsible for the debts/profits/losses/ taxation etc...
- **One Person Company**
  An extension of the sole proprietor form of business that

integrates the corporate framework. This results in the ability to form a company with limited liability i.e., the risks are limited to the value of shares held by the proprietor in the company.

- **Partnership**
This legal entity is formed between persons who have agreed to work together and take share in the profits of a business. The operations/decisions of the business are carried out based on mutual agreements between the partners.

- **Limited Liability Partnership (LLP)**
This type of partnership is a combination between a company and a partnership firm. The liability of the partners in LLP is confined to a limit. Unlike in a partnership, the partners in LLP are not liable for the acts of the other partners.

USA

For the USA, the legal entities that a start up may register as are slightly different from those discussed previously. The differences are given below.

- **Sole Proprietorship**
The business is owned and controlled exclusively by one person who is responsible for the business, entirety of the liability and the profits or losses.

- **Partnership**
Association of two or more people taking pre-decided part in profits and losses.

  - **General Partnership**
  Most basic type, assuming equal partnership and consequently equal ownership.

  - **Limited Partnership (Partnership with Limited Liability)**
  One or more of the partners manage the business and are

liable for the debts. This is decided based on mutual understanding as to which partner(s) is responsible for which/how much.

- ○ **Joint Venture**
  A time-based partnership that allows the individuals to work together for a particular project or for an extension of time. Upon completion of the time/project, the partnership is dissolved.

- **Limited Liability Company**
  LLC is a hybrid of a corporation and a partnership as it limits personal liability and distributes the profits and losses to individuals.
- **Business Corporation**
  Established to carry out particular types of business or transactions in the broadest sense of the word. The entity itself is separate from its owners and continues till it is legally dissolved.

UK

Similar structure to those that have been defined previously. The finer details and distinctions may be explored on the respective websites (Of course, they are all inspired by each other).

- **Sole Trader**
- **Partnership**
- **Limited Liability Partnership**
- **Limited Company**

UAE

Again, similar names and structures. However, there are a couple of entities that are structured uniquely and those are elaborated in more detail.

- **Sole Proprietorship**
- **Limited Liability Company (LLC)**
- **Civil Company**
  Opened by people in professions such as a doctor, accountant, engineer and lawyer. This company may have partners and the work of the company may only be from professional business. This focusses on activities that are practiced by one or more natural persons defined as part of capital.
- **Private Shareholding Company**
- **Public Shareholding Company**
- **Partnership**
  Although, overall this type of entity is similar to those defined for other countries, there is a major difference. UAE national must be general partners and partners of other nationalities may be limited partners. The limited partners may not intervene in the management or administrative issues of the general partners.

  - **General Partnership**
  - **Limited Partnership**

- **Branch of Foreign Companies**
  This requires the company to have a UAE national and the branch is supposed to carry out the same work as that of the parent company.
- **Representative Office**
  This is not a business structure but is business activity that a branch may conduct. It is able to promote and market the parent company's business but does NOT conduct business operations.

Singapore

The descriptions for the entities are similar to those with similar names elaborated previously.

- **Sole proprietorship or Partnership**
- **Limited Partnership**
- **Limited Liability Partnership**
- **Company**

Make sure to check the respective documents needed for registration of these entities according to the laws of the country.

Other Licences and Registrations

Each type of legal entity requires a registration. Based on the country of origin, these requirements may differ in the documentation required.

The aspect that is common is that you must submit the details of the business you plan to register. This includes details on the name, owner/partners, initial share holding (if applicable), the area of the company (technology, retail etc...) and what tasks the company plans to carry out. This part has already been figured out and must be adjusted formally in the different requirements based on regulations.

Based on the type of legal entity and the nature of the work that would be done in the legal entity, other licences and registrations would be required. For an entire list of documents/licences, it is best to visit the websites of official governing bodies. It will give you a more customized idea of the process and the requirements.

Money that your start up makes, needs to go somewhere! As a legal entity, your start up would be able to opt for opening a unique bank account. Again, different types of documents would be required based on your location and the type of legal entity.

Incubation Centres & Start Up Initiatives

Most governments, to encourage start ups and make the process easier, offer support through different avenues such as Incubations Centres or Start Up focus programs. These hubs provide start ups with mentorship and support. This book discusses incubators in further sections. However, it is important to highlight few of the benefits you and your start up may receive upon registering with these places. The benefits, again, vary based on your country of origination and setup.

Generally, these initiatives and hubs focus on growth and success of start ups and offer a comprehensive set of resources which includes but is not limited to

- **Facilities & services** – anything required for an initial setup of your start up in terms of office spaces and respective facilities.
- **Mentorship** – This is an important one! Having experienced mentors to guide you in different business processes, is an exceptional benefit that can boost the growth of your start up and possibly save you from few pitfalls.
- **Subsidies and Taxation Relief** – Based on fulfilling pre-requisites, your start up may be eligible for Government subsidies and taxation.
- **Funding** – Every start up needs initial funding to get started, whether its for production, marketing, or any other significant aspects. Government supported initiatives are essential and great first steps towards obtaining that funding.

Countries all over the world, offer such initiatives and centres. This includes the ATAL Incubation Centres in India, Start Up India program in India; Dcode and Blue Star Innovation Partners in USA, Cyberport in Hong Kong; UK Business Incubation (UKBI) in UK that brings together all initiatives. It is to note that each country has its own set of initiatives and centres. It is in the benefit of the founder to explore these services to find applicable subsidies and taxations.

Protection of Intellectual Property (IP)

You are offering your consumers a unique idea – whether that is a service or product, or both. Anything that a person creates - inventions, literary works, designs, logos, names and images, fall in the category of intellectual property. For example, if you have developed a unique logo for *MyStartUp*, then that logo is an intellectual property. This may be claimed as such legally for your company or yourself. Similarly, any written work, inventions etc... may all be categorized under IP and protected from others copying it or claiming it as their by registering under the suitable IP.

Trademark – Usually seen with a TM over a name or logo. This may be done for **a word, phrase, symbol or design**. It may also be done for a combination for the above mentioned items. It allows your customers to identify you and recognize you in the market.

Copyright – Issued for artistic creations, literary works. Now this includes everything from music to educational content, to art forms, artistic creations and more. A copyright gives permission to its owner to freely use, distribute that content.

Patent Registration – The most important form of IP that protects inventions and product creations. These are granted to the invention for a set period and give sole privileges to the owner of the patent in terms of the invention's terms of use.

Obtaining one or more of these falls under "protecting intellectual property". Depending on the type of IP, it can be a source of income for your business through licensing, sale or commercialization of protected designs and products. Furthermore, they also add value when you are trying to raise funding for your business .

CHAPTER VIII

Build Your Team

A great team is what takes a start up and elevates it towards its most successful form. Really! People who are working for the start up are the most essential contributors towards the success of your company. A start up may initially just begin with the founders and few key members. A good team will be a definite boon as the start up expands.

Finding the right team is sometimes a more challenging task than finding financing. It is important to realize that as you are just starting out, chances are that you are going to have a handful of employees. It is not about wanting to manage and hire many employees, but the right employees that are willing to do the work.

There are a few key points in the process of building initial teams for any start up. Let's detail them out. Here we go!

1. **Understand the Goal/ Vision**
   Whether you call it your company's vision, or its goals, future, plan...however you want to describe it, each member of your company should understand it, believe in it, and, most importantly, actively work towards achieving it.

   As the leader here, it is your responsibility to ensure that your vision is clearly communicated to all and is understood at the same level.

2. **Know what YOU (the owner) need**
   Only take the people you need. You will want to include your friends, family, the people you like and people who need help, and that's great. However, this is something you should do when you become an established company with more steady finances.

Initially, really focus on the key roles and tasks that are ESSENTIAL for your start up to take off. People who either understand the work that you do or are consistently interested in putting efforts and time towards the work.

3. **Hire for the Long term!**

   The team that you are building now at the beginning, is going to be the one that will know the innermost workings of your company. They will be the CORE team. Generally, the core team consists of the leaders of the company that contribute in the operations of the company. If you hire for the long term, you will not have to search for the correct people when you are a full-on business.

4. **Attitude is a double edged sword!**

   The right attitude can propel work and tasks forward at a greater speed than anticipated. However, a negative and contradictory attitude that inhibits the employees to work together would result in lesser efficiencies and work. Even more than skill sometimes, a person's attitude is an important factor in the ways they contribute to the team.

5. **Building a Team – The Hiring Process**

   It is not just hiring many people that fit the descriptions on paper, but it is about building a team that can work cohesively. Everybody will not get along with everybody else a 100%. However, your want to have people that are comfortably able to work with each other and are excited to work for a common vision/goal.

   This is where the hiring process must be thorough. Browse different portals for potential teammates, go through LinkedIn profiles and your own network circle. With the latter, make sure that you (and they) rememeber that working for the start up extends beyond your personal connections.

In addition to the features and skills that are important for the working of your business, let us stress it again:

THE PEOPLE AND THEIR ATTITUDE MATTER!

Their attitude towards the work as well as towards each other is significantly important. The team dynamics play an important role towards decision making as well as overall efficiencies.

What role do you play?

You are the leader, and of course, it is the most important and definitely the most fun role of them all. The role carries severe responsibilities, but this is the role that takes the company forward, it is the idea generator, problem solver, crisis management role that will keep you on your toes. You have the job to guide your team and manage them. If the team is losing sight of the vision or is getting misdirected, it is your job to course correct and bring everyone back on track! This will keep you and the team grounded and careful in the tasks that are performed and the decisions that are made.

It may be overwhelming to realize that this is a lot of responsibility, and that is okay. It may be challenging and may feel scary, but definitely worth it to bring your vision to reality.

So, if you feel scared, find your courage and do it anyway! Remember...

"Courage is not the absence of fear, but is simply doing something in-spite of it!"

CHAPTER IX

Develop Your Product or Service

The primary outcome of your company may be a service or an invention/design that you would like to sell as a product. For both services and products, you can develop a prototype. Now this is something you would want to do between your idea and launch phase. See, a prototype allows you to test the actual working of your design.

What is a prototype? It is basically a preliminary version of your product, an expression of design intent. This is a step that will show you the pros, cons, and challenges that may pop up with your design and how conveniently it may be used. Prototype for a service would be about either testing the service on a small number of your target consumers or about testing an app-based service through an initial launch.

Prototyping allows you to carry out a test-run to see how the design concept performs and if people are successfully and conveniently able to use it. A term commonly used with prototypes is fidelity. Fidelity references the look-and-feel of the final product or service. In terms of fidelity, prototypes range between low fidelity (lo-fi) and high fidelity (hi-fi). It may vary from the final product in terms of the

- Visual design/ representation of service
- Content
- Interactivity

Low fidelity prototypes are quick and easy representation of the product or service. Which means that the look and feel of the product/ service may be different from the final envisioned product. However, the primary goal with lo-fi prototyping is to test the functionality of the product and service.

High-fidelity prototypes look and feel as similar to the actual product that is being launched and will reach the customer. These are created primarily when the team has an in-depth understanding of what to build and are about to test with real users or the decision-making entities.

Product as a Prototype

For physical products, there is a prototyping process. To be fair, the concepts may also be applied to service-based start ups as well.
Broadly speaking, prototype design follows these steps

1. Understanding the functioning and operations of products with similar designs. Also understand their flaws.
2. Initiate the idea on paper – draw all the pieces of the puzzle that will bring together this prototype.
3. There are different software that may help you design the prototype in. Of course, if/ as is needed, hire a professional to assist you in developing design models.
4. If possible, start with a handmade design of the product. This will be a great way to get feel of the future product and its design modifications (if any).
5. Now comes the tough part. Once you have made the design and instructions on the connectivity of the different parts of your product, now you find someone to build it. As you search for an appropriate option to create this prototype:

   - Inquire about the credentials of the prototype making companies
   - Ask for their previous experience/work.
   - Cost and expenses.
   - protect your design

6. That last point is so important, it needs to be repeated! Make sure to protect your design as you get your prototype made. This may be achieved through a non-disclosure agreement (NDA) or a Memorandum of Understanding (MOU). Or you may already have obtained a patent on your design, in which case it is already protected. However, it does not hurt to have a NDA signed regardless.

7. Once built, test your prototype, and see what changes (if any) you can make to improve its output/performance.

Depending on the services of the company and the nature of the product, the prototype development is an important part and should be carried out diligently. Consult with experts in the domain to get the best possible custom advice on how to go forward with your prototype design.

Service as a Prototype

It is easy to visualize how a product may be prototyped. Visualizing the same for a service or a digital product, is a bigger challenge. For a digital product, the prototype is a simulation of the final interaction between the users and the interface. This is going to build on the market research and validation and take it a step further. The pain points are now evaluated for the customers, as well as the stakeholders (founders, shareholders etc...).

Service Prototype communicates the service experience to the primary stakeholders.

The benefit of the service prototype is to improve the experience of an existing service or to create a new service from zero level. Basically, it allows the developers to test the service without investing time and money to build the real service. It allows the stakeholders to:

- Experience the service from the customer's point of view
- Market Validation
- Detail out the workings of the service with the employees that would be responsible for execution of it.

How to build a service prototype?
Answer the following questions:

1. **What should we test and why?** – Detail out the aspects that are to be focussed on in the prototype/test. This may contain upto 6 touchpoints (ways in which the customer interacts with the start up. This includes mobile apps, marketing initiatives, sales representatives etc). This allows to define:

    ○ The scope of the customer journey
    ○ Objective of involving each of the touchpoints
    ○ Scope of the study

2. **How to determine the fidelity of the service?** – This means how the service conveys the experience in look-and-feel.
3. **What tool will allow you to carry out this prototyping?**

For digital outlets like blogging, media portals etc... good assessors are also in terms of the traffic to the site and performance of individual pieces of news/articles. It is possible to evaluate and categorize different evaluations and gain insights on which part of the service is a better fit.

CHAPTER X

Emerging Technologies for Business

Growth in product development in technology has been significant. Technology in different forms is an integral part of the latest advancements in different sectors like Healthcare, transportation, aviation, architecture and several others. Technology is a tool that helps all industry segments.

Emerging Technologies

Any technology is considered to be emerging if either:

- The technology itself is new and is making an impact in different sectors
- The technology has existed for some time, but new applications are coming up for that technology.

The most impactful names in Emerging Technologies include Artificial Intelligence (AI), Blockchain, Augmented Reality/Virtual Reality (AR/VR), Internet of Things (IoT), 3D Printing, Web App Development, Process Automation, Cybersecurity, Genomics, BioTech, Agriculture Technology (AgTech), and many more. Would you have direct utility with all these technologies? Possibly not. However, they may be useful in enhancing and streamlining your work processes or give you an idea for your next product.

Let's talk about two of these technologies.

Artificial Intelligence (AI)

Artificial Intelligence is a technology that has been almost as popular of a term as start ups recently. Probably more. Believe it or not, in your everyday lives, you use AI. Whether it is in recommendation systems, voice assistants like Alexa, Siri, Google Assistant, Bixby, Cortana and other, OTT platforms like Netflix or Amazon Prime (they use the recommendation systems), YouTube, or just online shopping...AI is already everywhere.

AI is developed in such a way to mimic human intelligence. The unique aspect about human intelligence includes our ability to apply logic, reason and take decisions. This is what AI tries to copy with targeted goals. All of the applications of AI are currently a part of *Narrow AI*. This implies that the AI is focussed in one specific area. For AI to do this, the powerhouse is machine learning, natural language processing and machine intelligence.

So how may this be useful for you?

1. **Product/ Service Enhancement**
   Based on what your product or service is, AI may be a great tool to enhance the operations of the service or the design and functioning of the product. A great example of using AI for product enhancement is the wearable Healthtech that are prevalent. Think of a FitBit or any smart watch. The device is an enhancement to the existing watch technology and offers applications that allow for health monitoring on the go.
2. **Analysis through data analytics**
   Data analytics have existed for a long time and offer great value to business owners. These insights are useful for companies to analyse and discern any drawbacks and contingencies. Now think of going beyond just insights towards the possibility of predictions (what customers are more likely to buy), detect fraud in real-time, analysis of warranty data to identify and maintain safety and quality in production. The list actually is endless...

All of this may be done through advanced algorithms and the

utility of existing or collected data.

3. **Business optimization applications**

AI applications have the potential to enhance the working of your business. It is not that AI would be a part of the product but a part of your inner workings. Let's see how that may be possible.

a. **Workflow Optimization**

For any business, documentation is important. Furthermore, task assignment and its follow through are something that may be tracked through AI Applications.

b. **Chatbots & Cognitive engagement.**

Chatbots and voice chatbots may be developed such that they are able to engage employees and customers using natural language processing, intelligent agents and machine learning.

c. **Process Automation**

Automation of digital and physical tasks, like back-office administrative and financial activities would free up your staff to do more intelligent work themselves. This includes automated e-mail responses, updating customer files, providing customer documentation, and reading legal documents. Of course, there are other applications that may be explored.

Although, the applications have been categorized, keep in mind that they are inter-related and support each other. Ultimately, this results in better customer care and service. Considering that you are starting with your business, possibly with limited people resources, exploring Artificial Intelligence solutions for Business Enhancement may allow you to allocate human resources to more smart tasks.

Web Development & Web App Development

While coming up with a name for your start up, there was also a mention of registering your business website domain as well. Once you have registered your domain, you have to think about hosting that website. Whether you decide to go for free registration/web hosting or paid, that is your choice. However, paid versions will allow you to have a unique and customized domain whereas the free versions will result in less cost but more generic web addresses that may not be easy to remember (no matter how good your company name is).

Let's talk about **Web Development.** It is the process that includes all actions, updates and operations that are a part of building, managing and maintaining a website. Designing your start up's website is an important task. There are different technologies that you can use to develop a custom website. Before you do that, let's understand a few commonly used terms.

- **Back-end and Front-end**
  Front-end refers to the client side of the website or the software. This is the part that the user sees and interacts with – playing videos, view images, highlighting text etc...

  Back-end refers to the server-side of things with which the users do not interact. This is the digital infrastructure which stores and manages data. The back-end is not seen by the users.
- **Static and Dynamic Websites**
  Static Websites offer stable content which remains the same for every user that opens the website. This page is created using HTML, CSS and Javascript (web development languages) and a change to the website would require a change to the code. Examples of such websites include those of universities and other organizations.

A **Dynamic website** is more custom for the user. It delivers and displays the content according to user behavior or based on user-generated content. It allows you, as the business owner, to customize and personalize the website experience for your users. Think of social media platforms or news platforms, where the content is customized according to user preferences.

The technologies for web development are evolving. A few of these technologies and languages are as follows:

- HTML, CSS,JavaScript Web APIs
- Node.js
- jQuery
- Angular
- React.js
- Vue.js
- Ruby on Rails

If you are not looking into coding/ programming, then try the drag and drop web development options like Wix, Wordpress, Mobirise. These options also offer hosting services. Now, if you have an idea for your website, but are unsure of the layout and/ or of devoting the time commitment required, then there are other businesses, freelancers and start ups that offer services to create your websites with the latest designs and frameworks.

Web App Development

A Web App is an interactive web based application which the users are able to access through their browser, basically like a website. So is it the same as a website? No! Web App Development and Web Development share many characteristics. Both in front-end and back-end execution. The difference, however, is that a Web App is interactive whereas the primary goal of a website is to share information.

Progressive Web Apps (PWAs) are easily downloaded to a user's device (like an Android or iOS app) and do not need a browser to launch. Also, they can work offline and operate fairly quickly. They are installable, responsive, and safe. In other words, they are "traditional websites in mobile app packaging".

There are quite a few benefits of web development for every start up. Similarly, Web Apps offer several distinct benefits as well:

- **Portability** – the user is able to access the app from any device, ranging from a laptop to a tablet. They are multi-platform and provide the users with the option to utilize the app without any limitation of the operating system.
- **Convenience** – the Web Apps do not need to be downloaded and installed. They will run on the browser (regardless of which one it is). PWAs may be downloaded on the device but do not require too many of the resources.
- **Competitive Edge** – In today's market, web apps are an essential tool to keep customers. These apps are a great avenue to sell goods and interact with their clients. Furthermore, the monetization may also be in terms of membership fees, dues or ads.
- **Security** – Web Apps can protect websites and software programs as they are designed for more privacy and higher levels of security.

Consider any e-commerce and web apps. E-commerce is a software application where both the buyer and seller can interact for purchase and selling of different items. E-Commerce platforms may be customized to your business, or you may develop a unique E-commerce platform which others can utilize to sell their own products. A great example of this is Etsy which is a platform that allows artists and small-scale craftspeople to share their unique products. The company earns through a small service fee that is levied on each showcased product.

Although only two major segments of technologies have been discussed here, it may be in your benefit to explore other technologies, both, in terms of utility to your start up and new product ideas.

CHAPTER XI

Brand Your Business and Advertise

Before you start selling your product and service, it is good to get started on building your brand and increasing your reach (or your following). This is a great way to introduce your potential customers to your products and get them excited to choose your products and services. So instead of you searching for customers, the customers would be searching for you! Perfect!

The age old clarification – branding vs marketing.

Branding and marketing are two essential aspects of taking your product/service to the market. They also represent different, but related things. Another term you commonly hear is advertising. So let's briefly understand what they are.

Branding is all about who you are – your principles and values, your mission statements, motivation behind building your business. Ask yourself the following questions and you will gain a better understanding of your brand and its values.

- What are the core values, principles and morals of my start up?
- What is the mission and vision?
- What is the motivation behind addressing this problem or building this business?
- What makes my business unique? What do I want people to instantly think of when they hear our name? Is it trust, loyalty, knowledgeable, or some other emotion entirely?

Answering these questions elaborately will help you understand more about what value you actually want to carry forward and will also be able to explain it to your team. This is directly going to develop the perception that your customers will develop for you, your products, and services.

In comparison, what is marketing? **Marketing** refers to the tools that are used to showcase and deliver the brand's message and value to the consumers. Whereas the brand values will stay rigid and the same, the marketing will evolve, based on the product/services and any changes you introduce. Marketing is done to directly reach your target audience, all the while supporting the core values that are the essence of your brand.

Marketing is done to get people excited, even before the launch of your product. However, it is not just about getting people excited about the initial launch but to maintain that momentum and level of interest in your brand. Therefore, develop a well-rounded marketing strategy. Marketing includes utilizing all possible avenues to increase product/service visibility and brand value. This includes traditional methods of magazines, news papers and other print material, as well as digital media, social media, and websites.

What is a part of Marketing?

Based on the product/service and the target audience, you will have to figure out whether traditional or digital marketing tools will be better for you, in terms of local reach. However, if you are looking at reaching clients beyond your immediate neighbourhood, then digital marketing is your way to go.

1. **<u>Logo</u>**

   Logos are a brand representation that can be utilized anywhere and everywhere – whether business cards, letterheads, print media, websites, social media platforms and much more. Your logo essentially is your biggest brand representative and potential clients will start recognizing you with it. In a lot of cases, logos are bigger representatives than companies themselves.

For example, more people may recognize the *hp*logo but they may not entirely know that it stands for Hewlett & Packard, the founders of the company. Having an attractive logo design that is unique, adds to your intellectual property and also showcases your brand.

2. **<u>Website – Personal or Company</u>**
The most basic form of online presence, a website builds trust and is a central location that is just about YOUR business and product. On your website, you can introduce people to your brand, your products and showcase your unique selling points (USP).

Many customers will check online for any new company they hear about.

3. **<u>Google Services</u>**
List your business on Google. This is a great way to pop-up in searches when people are either 1) searching for your brand or product
2) are looking for something with similar application and/or name.
It provides an easy summary of your services and gives an overview of customer feedback.

4. **<u>Social Media</u>**
Think about where you are most likely to be introduced to new product lines in today's social media infused world? Majority of information about new products and lines is now on the most popular social media platforms like Instagram, Facebook, Pinterest, LinkedIn and few others. Although, these social media handles may not always result in direct customer conversion, they allow for directly interacting with them, more so than any other marketing avenue.

These platforms may be used to simply share how something about your service works or may showcase new product launch, discounts, direct interaction....there are so many ways to interact directly with your customer base. Remember, each follower may be counted as a potential client.

5. **<u>Print and Digital Media</u>**

   Traditionally, newspapers and magazines have always brought about news and the latest happenings across the globe. Now that job is also being taken care by digital media print houses. The reach of digital media is greater. Even the traditional media houses have a copy available online. Considering the ad spaces available on these media house pages (both web and physical), think of how you can advertise your product/services through them.

6. **<u>Customer Service Software</u>**

   CRM software solutions allow you to store customer data so as to improve how you may modify and develop your marketing strategy. Email marketing, or in today's world, even marketing through social chat platforms like WhatsApp can also increase your reach.

   Don't forget that traditional methods of providing customer care are not only still valid, but they are assumed to be active for any company.

There are several different avenues where you can market your product/services and brand. Think about the target customer that you would like to approach and what they access more. Invest in these marketing outlets accordingly.

For any start up, managing the available funds is a big challenge.

As you develop your marketing strategy, also develop the corresponding budgeting for the different avenues. A part of this will be a learn-as-you-go. More marketing avenues you try, you will gain a better understanding of what methodology is resulting in real visibility to client and, more importantly client conversion.

Remember, visibility is important. However, the revenue will come in with client conversion.

CHAPTER XII

Finance Your Business: Start Up Funding

The money details! Finally, you get to talk about finances. Basically, money stuff.

While talking about finances, there are two major aspects that should be considered for any start up: 1) Acquiring funds 2) Managing Finances. Both are significant for smooth operations of your start up. Managing finances is primarily concerned with keeping track of all expenses and incoming revenues. As an entrepreneur, it is imperative to understand basic financial aspects and its management. Of course, you can always hire another person/entity to manage your finances, but you should still have a fundamental know-how of how they work.

Now, acquiring the funds – this is how you source the money to set up and conduct the operations of your business. There are several different financial models that are available for all start ups and businesses. You have the option to follow one or more, based on your requirements, and as time goes by, you also have the option to modify that financial model.

Let's see the options now!

- **<u>Family financing – Talk to the people closest to you</u>**
  It is initially a bit challenging to find the right source of funding for the start up and this is where borrowing directly from friends and family can be beneficial. There may also be more manageable interest rates and more comfortable payment options. However, be aware that money can be the cause of conflicts and you should avoid getting to that stage with loved ones.
- **<u>Personal Credit Lines</u>**
  The easiest and most convenient way to get started. A *personal credit line* or *personal loan* is basically a loan that you can take

out from any lender, like a bank. These funds remain available to you and you may use them as you need.

Since this is a loan, you would have to make regular payments to return the amount back to your lender over a specific period of time. Also, let's not forget about the interest rates, which are higher are on personal loans. It is a good option for obtaining initial funds for your start up but make sure to have quick returns in order to pay back the loan.

<u>Apply for Business Loans</u>

Small Business Loans are an option that you may get through any local or major banks. Like any loan, it is paid back at a particular interest rate and over a period. These details are fixed between the lender institute (bank) and the lendee (you)!

What makes this different from a personal credit line is the collateral. What is collateral? It is something that you put up as a security for repayment of a loan. This means that in case you are unable to pay back the amount and interest of the loan, then whatever collateral you have put up, would be surrendered to the bank.

In other words, you have to give up what you put as collateral in case of failure to pay back the money. Okay, so that sounds scary but it is not something you should be afraid of. The payment plan may be customized and is easy to manage as long as you have revenue coming in.

Let's talk about who you can obtain this loan from:

- ◦ Banks, Credit Unions – They provide a lot of options which may customized according to your needs.

- ○ Online Lenders – If you do not want to put up a collateral, then you may also search for investors online that may directly be able to help your business.
- ○ Non-profit microlenders – Smaller lenders may be a source of getting a loan, specially in the case where your start or company is smaller in size.

Usually, when you apply for a loan, these organizations/individual lenders are interested in seeing a business plan (Good thing you have that ready already!). Even within your business plan, they are more interested in seeing **financial numbers (finance plan), Steps/ Process to growth, Mission/Vision Statements, Product/ service descriptions, About the Company (leadership, origin, existing team).**

Angel Investors – Boon for start ups

Angel Investors are basically private investors that can be a source of capital for your start up. Usually these investors use their personal funds to contribute to your start up and business idea.

Note how the term being used here is investment and not loan with reference to obtaining funds from Angel Investors. This is because, unlike banks and venture capitalists, angel investors do not require the amount to be paid back. Angel investment works with an exchange of equity for the amount they are investing. So the investor owns a stake in your company and is entitled to a part of your profits.

A great example of this is the show *Shark Tank* where business owners have the ability to pitch directly to investors. Watching similar programs is a great way to understand how Angel Investors can work and help.

Again, a business plan is of great help here.

Venture Capitalists

These are private investors that are interested in providing financial services and funding to start ups and businesses. Now here, the lenders are already working together in a Limited Partnership (LP) and together invest in one collective fund. These funds are then issued/ distributed to different businesses as approved.

This is one of the main differences between venture capitalists and angel investors.

Here, a business plan along with an idea of how much equity you are willing to give up are essential information to have, before you talk with VCs. Also, VCs are more interested if you have moved beyond just the idea of your business and are into product/service launch.

Incubator cells – public and privately owned

Incubators are hubs that offers support and initial facilities to young companies and start ups. It can offer funding as well as mentorship and different tools that you may need for your start up. Now this can be something like equipment or it can be something else like legal or accounting consultancy/ services. Overall Incubation cells are a source for mentorship and guidance for a start up and offer group learning options. Different countries house their own incubator cells. For example, Hub71, In5, Dtec and Wamda are great examples of Incubation Cells in Dubai. In India, Sine, STEp, CIEIIMA, pupilfirst, all fall in the Top 10 Incubations Centre lists. Then there are incubators in North America (US and Canada) which includes places like Techstars, Capital Factory, Mucker Lab, Angel Pad and many more. Similarly, BLOCK71 is a leading Incubator in Singapore.

Utilizing government grants and subsidies

Globally, governments are encouraging start ups and small businesses. They do so in the form of grants and subsidies. There may be conditions on who can apply or qualify for these grants. For example, a certain subsidy may only be applicable if your start up focusses on Science & Technology or Creative Arts.

Keeping an eye out for these grants and subsidies is important as they are a big boost to the financial structure of the company and don't require payments to be returned.

These have been a few sources of obtaining the funds. There are options to directly raise funds from the public. This has its benefits as it also gives you the freedom to directly communicate (via a platform or through communicative material) with people (who may or may not be your potential client base) about your start up. Now let's talk about ways how you can directly raise funds from the people:

Crowdfunding

This initiative gives the option to raise small amounts of money for your business which can be used for daily operations of the company. Here, you are appealing directly to your customer base/ the population to offer a small amount of money to sustain your business.

Now your pitch here is going to be a bit different from the business plan you presented to the angel investors and the venture capitalists. Here you appeal directly to your *audience,* and can share your crowdfunding campaign on different *public and social media* platforms to increase its reach. It is important in crowdfunding to pick the right platform and using targeted marketing materials.

<u>Peer-to-peer lending</u>

Another way to explain Peer-to-peer lending is that you are primarily obtaining your funding from other businesses and lenders. Again, you can try different platforms that offer these services (like Funding Circle) and avail unique benefits of lower interest rates and flexibility in usage. However, there are limitations to how much you can borrow. These platforms are also a great way to provide funding to other businesses when you feel yours is financially stable.

Before deciding on your finance model, understand how and when you're going to need the finances. Keep in mind, this is something you have tentatively included in your business plan. Something like Crowdfunding has the option of more endless funding without having to pay the amount back, but this can also be a slower way of raising the amount. Therefore, having a clear idea of your spending and financial needs is necessary. The finance plan will help you in gaining an understanding of when and how you will need to distribute the finances, and therefore, an understanding of when and how you will need the money.

Stages of Funding

So far, the focus has been on how to get different aspects of a start up moving forward. If and when everything works right, every start up should also think about taking the business to the next level.

In addition to different ways and sources of obtaining funding, there are different stages of funding that apply to start ups.

1. **<u>Pre-seed funding stage</u>**

   Research phase of initiating your start up. Look to find answer to the following key aspects:

   - Is the idea valid – is it viable?
   - Does the same solution to a problem already exist?
   - How cost effective will this venture be?
   - Which financial model have you chosen? Which business structure (Proprietorship, pvt ltd company) have you opted for?
   - What is the first step? Also, what is the next step after that?

   The goal with the last question is to develop a set of processes for you to follow as you venture into your own business. Source of funds in this area is usually friends and family or personal loans.

2. **<u>Seed Funding Stage</u>**

   In this stage, your idea is already a business. Meaning you have launched your start up and have a customer base ready. Gaining funding from investors in this phase concerns with offering equity in exchange for more significant financial aid. Generally, the funds can contribute to product launch, marketing strategies, research and new employees. Start thinking about growth options for your company.

3. **<u>Series A Funding</u>**

   This stage of funding is where the venture capital investments begin. Shares of the company become the exchange currency in return for the funds. Here the funds are utilized to optimize the business processes and manage any financial challenges. This also gives an opportunity to improve on the existing products.

4. **<u>Series B Funding</u>**

    By this stage of funding, it is expected that your start up has a dedicated user base and a steady incoming revenue from your products and services. Now start thinking about scaling through doing market research activities again and increasing your market share. Now is generally when start ups form teams dedicatedly operating for business development and marketing. Again, this may already exist in your business due to the nature of your product/services.

5. **<u>Series C Funding</u>**

    A start up looking at this stage of funding may be considering large scale expansion, maybe even globally. You would have the option to build new products and/or reach new markets with the funding you receive from investors.

6. **<u>Series D Funding & more</u>**

    Beyond this round of funding, the start up is looking at utilizing the funds to explore new opportunities or correct issues caused due to inadequate performance in the previous segments.

7. **<u>Bridge Loans</u>**

    Designed for fairly mature start ups that ae rapidly expanding and playing in greater amounts of money.

8. **<u>IPO</u>**

    This is the ultimate stage where all start ups want to reach. This is when the shares of the start up are offered to the public for purchasing for the first time.

Now, these are different stages of funding to give you a measure of where your start up fits in right now. These are guidelines – do remember. Regularly carrying out the evaluation of your start up is an informative technique to quantify the worth of a company. This is also called a valuation process.

The valuation of a company is an important aspect as it gives the owner (you) an idea of how much equity you should give to an investor. For the same reason, it is important to the investor as well. There are different factors based on which the evaluation of your start up will take place. This includes the existence of demand of your product/service; image in the market; developed prototype (this is very important); available and potential distribution channels; pre-valuation revenues; and which industry your start up is in. Once you have these parameters in hand, there are different models that you can use for the valuation of your start up.

You are just starting out, so stay focussed and do not forget the reason for starting something of your own. Getting started early with your entrepreneurship journey will give you an understanding of how the financial and corporate aspects function. As you plan to do this while managing prior commitments, stay honest to your work, your timelines and the goals you want to achieve.

Keep your passion alive and keep that creativity flowing!

9 7 9 8 8 8 8 1 5 8 5 4 8